Fact Finders™

Questions and Answers: Countries

India

A Question and Answer Book

by Nathan Olson

WITHDRAWN

Consultant:
Philip K. Oldenburg, PhD
Adjunct Research Associate
Southern Asia Institute, Columbia University
New York, New York

Capstone
press

Mankato, Minnesota

Fact Finders is published by Capstone Press,
151 Good Counsel Drive, P.O. Box 669, Mankato, Minnesota 56002.
www.capstonepress.com

Library of Congress Cataloging-in-Publication Data
Olson, Nathan.
    India: a question and answer book / by Nathan Olson.
    p. cm.—(Fact finders. Questions and answers. Countries)
    Includes bibliographical references and index.
    ISBN 0-7368-3751-5 (hardcover)
    1. India—Juvenile literature. I. Title. II. Series.
DS407.O47 2005
954—dc22   2004011304

Summary: Describes the geography, history, economy, and culture of India in a
    question-and-answer format.

Editorial Credits
Megan Schoeneberger, editor; Kia Adams, set designer; Kate Opseth, book designer; Nancy
    Steers, map illustrator; Wanda Winch, photo researcher; Scott Thoms, photo editor

Photo Credits
Corbis/Jeremy Horner, 15; Lindsay Hebberd, 23
Corel, 1
Cory Langley, cover (foreground), 4, 12–13
Digital Vision, 24
Doranne Jacobson, 11, 16, 16–17, 18–19, 25, 27
Flat Earth, 20
Getty Images Inc./AFP/Prakash Singh, 9; Central Press, 7
Photo courtesy of Paul Baker, 29 (coins)
Photo courtesy of Richard Sutherland, 29 (bill)
Photodisc/Ingo Jezierski, cover (background)
Root Resources/Claudia Adams, 21
StockHaus Ltd., 29 (flag)

Artistic Effects
Ingram Publishing, 12; Photodisc/Siede Preis, 8

1 2 3 4 5 6 10 09 08 07 06 05

Table of Contents

Features

Where is India?

India is a large country in southern Asia. It is almost twice the size of Alaska.

India has many mountains. The peaks of the Himalaya form part of India's northeast border. These mountains are some of the tallest in the world. The Western and Eastern Ghats stand along India's coasts.

Boats travel on India's rivers and lakes. ➤

4

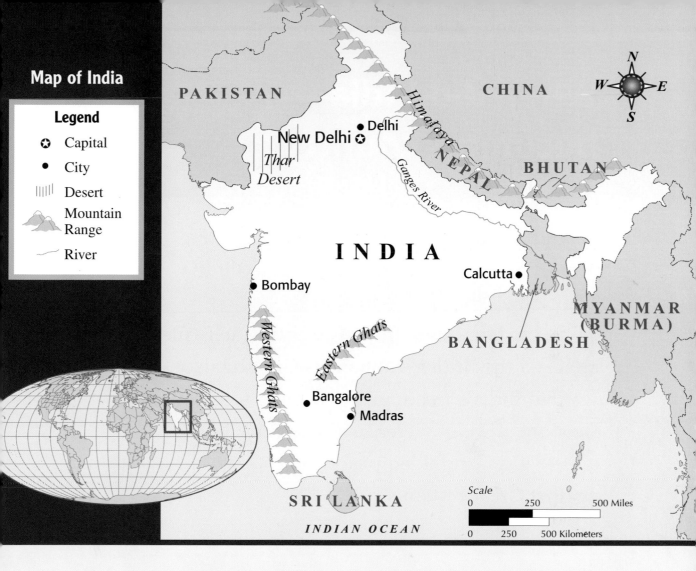

Map of India

Legend
- ✪ Capital
- ● City
- |||| Desert
- 🏔 Mountain Range
- ∼ River

PAKISTAN

CHINA

Thar Desert

New Delhi ✪ ● Delhi

Himalaya

NEPAL

BHUTAN

Ganges River

INDIA

Bombay ●

Calcutta ●

BANGLADESH

MYANMAR (BURMA)

Western Ghats

Eastern Ghats

Bangalore ●

Madras ●

SRI LANKA

INDIAN OCEAN

Scale
0   250   500 Miles
0   250   500 Kilometers

Other land features cover the rest of
India. Rivers flow through India's plains.
The Ganges River brings water for farming.
Thick forests cover parts of central and
western India. The hot and dry Thar Desert
reaches to India's border with Pakistan.

When did India become a country?

India became its own country in 1947. From 1757 to 1947, Great Britain ruled India. They called the land British India.

In the late 1800s, Indians wanting self-rule attacked the British. Mohandas Gandhi also wanted India's freedom. He wanted to gain freedom without violence. During the 1930s and 1940s, Gandhi led peaceful protests against Great Britain's rule.

Fact!

In the mid-1960s, many Americans copied the style of jacket worn by Jawaharlal Nehru, India's first prime minister. Americans called it a Nehru jacket.

Jawaharlal Nehru (left) and Mohandas Gandhi (right) discuss India's freedom. Nehru became India's first prime minister.

In 1947, the British left India. British India was divided into India and Pakistan. People of the Hindu and Sikh religions stayed in India. Pakistan became the homeland for most of the Muslims of British India.

What type of government does India have?

India's government is a **federal republic**. A national government runs the country. India is divided into states. Each state has its own chief minister and legislature.

India has a **prime minister** and a **parliament**. The prime minister works with the parliament to run India's government. The parliament makes laws. The Council of States and the House of the People make up India's parliament.

Fact!

India's parliament has up to 795 members. This number is 260 more than the U.S. Congress, which has 535 members.

Members of India's House of the People meet to discuss laws.

India holds a national election about every five years. Indians vote for a political party. The leader of the winning party becomes the prime minister.

What kind of housing does India have?

Most Indians live in villages. They build small houses out of clay, brick, and palm leaves. Most rural homes do not have running water. Families get water from the village well.

Many Indians in cities live in small houses or apartment buildings. These homes have running water.

Where do people in India live?

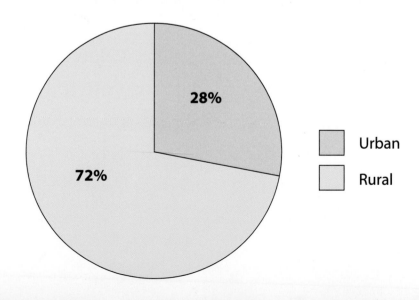

28%

72%

Urban

Rural

Villagers carry pots of water to their homes.

Some Indians without much money live in shelters made out of cardboard and scrap metal. They build the shelters near each other to form small towns. People call these towns shantytowns. Shantytowns are often built in cities.

What are India's forms of transportation?

Many Indians ride motorcycles or bicycles. They also travel by **cycle rickshaw** or taxi. Many people ride on buses. Buses are very crowded. Some people ride by hanging on to the outside of buses. Few Indians own cars.

India's train system allows people to travel across the country. It is the largest train system in Asia. Trains stop in many Indian cities.

Fact!

Cows often wander India's city streets. In India, killing a cow is a serious crime. Drivers must stop for cows on streets.

Cycle rickshaws are the cheapest way to travel in some cities.

In rural areas, most roads are too bumpy for cars. Instead, people ride bicycles or motor scooters. They also ride in carts pulled by oxen or horses.

What are India's major industries?

Farming and fishing are important to India's **economy**. Farmers grow rice and wheat. They use oxen and tractors to plow their fields. Many farmers raise water buffalo for milk. People also fish for shrimp off India's coasts. Some people use large wells and village ponds to raise fish to eat.

India's land is rich in **natural resources**. Companies drill for oil in northeastern India. Indians also mine coal and iron ore.

What does India import and export?	
Imports	*Exports*
nonelectrical machinery	*engineering products*
oil and oil products	*gems and jewelry*
precious stones	*textiles*

Fabrics hang on racks to dry at an Indian textile factory.

Indian factories make many goods. **Textile** factories make clothing out of cotton or silk. Other factories make steel and iron. Indian companies also make bicycles and computers.

What is school like in India?

In India, the school day begins at 8:00 in the morning. Young students go home at lunchtime. After lunch, older students stay for classes until 3:00 in the afternoon. Some students learn in classrooms with desks. Other students sit on mats on the floor. Children study history, math, and geography.

Students in a rural school sit on the floor while doing schoolwork. ➤

In some classrooms, students share desks.

Indians go to grade school between the ages of 6 and 10. They attend middle school until they are 14 years old. Indian law says that children must finish middle school. Many students choose to attend secondary school after middle school.

What are India's favorite sports and games?

Indian men often play a game called *kabaddi*. In this game, two teams each take a side of a playing field. One player crosses the center line and tries to tag as many players as possible. He then tries to return to his side. The other team tries to stop him. If the player is able to return, his team scores. If he doesn't, the other team scores.

Fact!

A kabaddi *player must tag the other players and return to his side without taking a breath. He proves that he is not taking a breath by shouting* "kabaddi, kabaddi, kabaddi" *as he runs.*

Boys play a game of cricket.
Cricket is like baseball.

Indians play many other sports. **Cricket** is India's most popular sport. Field hockey is India's national sport. Indians learned these sports from the British. Indians also play volleyball and soccer.

What are the traditional art forms in India?

Architecture is one of India's oldest art forms. Palaces, temples, and statues fill Indian cities. The Taj Mahal is India's most famous building. In the 1600s, an emperor ordered workers to build the Taj Mahal as a tomb for his favorite wife.

The Taj Mahal stands in Agra, India. The building took about 20,000 workers and hundreds of elephants 22 years to finish. ➤

A woman dances at a festival in northern India.

Music and dance are part of Indian life. The sitar and *tanpura* are Indian instruments. They look like long guitars. Dancers in fancy costumes perform traditional dances. They tell stories through their movements.

What major holidays do people in India celebrate?

Many of India's holidays come from the Hindu religion. Diwali is the festival of lights. People clean their homes and exchange candy. During Holi, Hindus celebrate spring. The Holi celebration is also called the Festival of Color. People throw colored water and powder at each other to honor the colors of nature.

Muslim Indians celebrate Islamic holidays. Ramadan lasts for 30 days. During Ramadan, Muslims do not eat or drink during daylight hours. They pray for much of the day.

What other holidays do people in India celebrate?

Christmas Day
Dussehra
Gandhi's Birthday
Nehru's Birthday

Colorful powder and water covers the crowds of people celebrating Holi.

Indians also celebrate national holidays. January 26 is Republic Day. Independence Day is August 15. People go to parades and festivals on these days.

What are the traditional foods of India?

In India, religion affects what people eat. Hindus do not eat beef. Muslims do not eat pork. Instead, Indians eat goat, chicken, and vegetables. They season their food in a spicy, creamy stew called **curry**. Some Indians serve curries with rice. Others scoop their curries with a flat bread called chapati.

Fact!

India is famous for spices like cinnamon, pepper, and ginger. In the 1600s, many explorers traveled to India to find spices.

Indians often sit on the floor during meals.

For most Indians, lunch is the largest meal of the day. For lunch, Indians eat curries with rice and bread. Breakfast and supper are smaller meals. They usually include bread, yogurt, and vegetables. Indians drink tea or coffee between meals.

What is family life like in India?

In the past, India had a **caste** system. Castes divided the rich from the poor. Lower caste people couldn't eat, live, or pray with higher caste people. Today, the government gives people equal rights. But many people still follow the caste system. Most Indians will marry only people from their own caste.

What are the ethnic backgrounds of people in India?

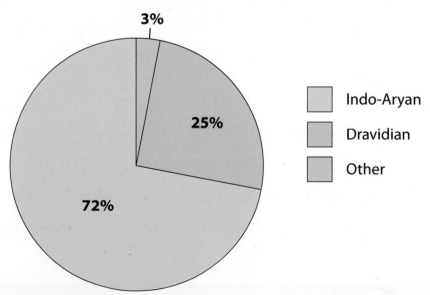

3%

25%

72%

Indo-Aryan

Dravidian

Other

An Indian family celebrates a child's birthday with cakes and candles.

Parents play an important role in children's lives. Parents spoil their young children. Older children have more chores and responsibilities. In most families, parents choose whom their children will marry.

India Fast Facts

Official name:

Republic of India

Land area:

1,147,950 square miles
(2,973,191 square kilometers)

Average annual precipitation:

49 inches (124 centimeters)

Average January temperature (New Delhi):

57 degrees Fahrenheit
(14 degrees Celsius)

Average July temperature (New Delhi):

88 degrees Fahrenheit
(31 degrees Celsius)

Population:

1.05 billion people

Capital city:

New Delhi

Languages:

Hindi, English, and 16 other official languages

Natural resources:

farmland, forests, mica, oil, water

Religions:

Hindu	80.5%
Islamic	13.4%
Christian	2.3%
Sikh	1.9%
Buddhist	0.8%
Other	1.1%

Money and Flag

Money:

India's money is the Indian rupee. In 2004, 1 U.S. dollar equaled 45 Indian rupees. One Canadian dollar equaled 33 Indian rupees.

Flag:

India's flag has three stripes. Yellow-orange stands for strength. White means peace. Green stands for India's good farmland. In the center is a symbol called the Dharma Chakra.

Learn to Speak Hindi

Most people in India speak Hindi. It is one of India's official languages. Learn to speak some Hindi words using the chart below.

English	Hindi	Pronunciation
hello and good-bye	namaste	(nah-mah-stay)
yes	haan	(hahn)
no	nahin	(nah-heen)
thank you	dhanyavad	(don-yah-vahd)
How are you?	aap kaise hain	(ahp kess-eh hayn)

Glossary

architecture (AR-ki-tek-chur)—the planning and designing of buildings

caste (KAST)—a division of society based on differences of wealth, profession, occupation, or race

cricket (KRIK-it)—an outdoor game played by two teams of 11 players with flat bats and a hard ball

curry (KUH-ree)—an Indian food or sauce seasoned with a mixture of strong spices

cycle rickshaw (SYE-kuhl RIK-shaw)—a three-wheeled taxi for two passengers pedaled like a bicycle by a driver

economy (i-KON-uh-mee)—the way a country runs its industry, trade, and finance

federal republic (FED-ur-uhl ri-PUHB-lik)—a government of many states led by a president or prime minister with officials elected by voters

natural resource (NACH-ur-uhl REE-sorss)—a material found in nature that is useful to people

parliament (PAR-luh-muhnt)—the group of people who have been elected to make laws in some countries

prime minister (PRIME MIN-uh-stur)—the person in charge of a government in some countries

textile (TEK-stile)—a fabric or cloth that has been woven or knitted

Internet Sites

FactHound offers a safe, fun way to find Internet sites related to this book. All of the sites on FactHound have been researched by our staff.

Here's how:
1. Visit *www.facthound.com*
2. Type in this special code **0736837515** for age-appropriate sites. Or enter a search word related to this book for a more general search.
3. Click on the **Fetch It** button.

FactHound will fetch the best sites for you!

Read More

De Capua, Sarah. *India*. First Reports. Minneapolis: Compass Point Books, 2003.

Italia, Bob. *India.* The Countries. Edina, Minn.: Abdo, 2002.

Murphy, Patricia J. *India*. Discovering Cultures. New York: Benchmark Books, 2003.

Sapre, Reshma. *India.* Steadwell Books World Tour. Austin, Texas: Raintree Steck-Vaughn, 2002.

Index